Some Roads Lead To Somewhere.
Some Roads Lead To Someone.
2nd Edition

My Thoughts and Reflections on the Journey of Life

Dr. Rodel Aguas

Some Roads Lead to Somewhere. Some Roads Lead to Someone.

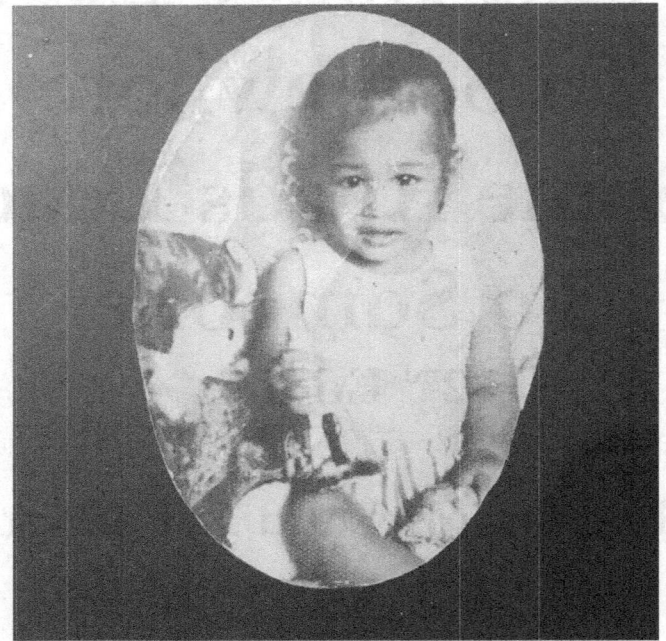

DEDICATION

To all my wonderful travel companions in my life 's journey especially my best travel partners: my beloved wife, Mila; my beautiful daughters - Frances, Pauleene, and Vikki; my wonderful sons-in law - Ronald, Ramoncito, and Martin; my cherished grandchildren - Rodel, Jiren, Dylan, Sophia, Martina, and Lennon; my noble father, Rogelio; my saintly mother – Jovita, my praiseworthy stepmother -Victoria; my admirable grandparents, in-laws, brothers and sisters, relatives and friends (especially Reverend Father William Au), I dedicate my treasured travel notes in this journey called "life" where I have learned to love and treasure you all.

And most of all to my amazing God - my Heavenly Father, my Brother Jesus, and my Best Friend, the Holy Spirit. I also thank my wonderful friends in Heaven, Mary our Mother, Saint Therese, and Saint Francis of Assisi who have inspired me in my journey and continue to stay in touch until I finally make it … Home.

CONTENTS

There are roads that lead somewhere ....

and there are roads that lead to someone.

Forward

This book is different from what you may have expected when you picked it up. It is the author's reflections on a variety of experiences ranging from his teaching career to the personal trauma of illness and relationship heartaches, to the deeper human questions in modern cinema. They are the reflections of a man whose mind and heart are always focused on how the ordinary events of our lives contain the ultimate challenges and lessons about what it means to be human, and how the heart can find peace and meaning if open to the ways love can be found and shared in all our human encounters and struggles.

Most of all they are the reflections of a man who learned how to be open to seeing the presence of God in all the events of his life and found the ultimate peace of discovering that the One his heart was always restless to find had already found him. At first, some readers may react to the situations cited and the truths expressed in these reflections as obvious. Yet think again and dive in deeper. For these reflections capture the wisdom of the hard-won discovery of finding in the most ordinary situations, simple joys and universal sufferings of life what is most important and gives life meaning.

I hope you will enjoy, as I did, reading these reflections and comparing them to your own experiences. For it is in telling our stories and sharing lessons learned and insights gained that we discover who we are and come to recognize ourselves in each other.

Reverend Father William A. Au, Ph.D.
Shrine of the Sacred Heart Parish Community
Baltimore, Maryland, USA
October 22, 2024

Prologue:

Some Roads Lead to Somewhere

I grew up in a village named after Saint Therese of Lisieux in San Fernando, the capital city of the province of Pampanga in the Philippines. Its old name was "Baritan" which was derived from the name of a species of grass, "barit", that grew in abundance near its creek. This "barit" was fed to horses that pulled the two – wheeled carriage, our local transportation called "calesa".

When I reached the age of six years old, I walked every school day to Saint Scholastica Academy, which was located in "Baritan" with my "yaya" (babysitter). After school, I walked home again with my "yaya". We walked that long road to and from the school, rain or shine. With my small steps, I was able to take a fifteen-minute walk one way. I usually play pranks with my yaya, like pretending to have tantrums so that she will let go of my hand, and then I would run ahead, leaving her behind. After that, I would wait at the gate of our house and tease her for walking too slowly. One day, I played the same prank with her, ran laughing, but this time fell into a ditch and was covered in mud. My 'yaya' laughed her heart out when she saw me. She pulled me out of the ditch and asked, "Silly boy, why did you run away from me?" Let's go home and I will clean you up." I learned my first lesson on the road that day, that I should not run away from the person who takes good care of me, lest I fall into a ditch.

Often, we take for granted people who genuinely care for us thinking we will be better off alone without them. Then we fall into the ditch of our foolishness and get ourselves muddied by our bad decisions. Much to our surprise and shame, the very people who pull us out of the ditch are the very same people we ran away from. These are the same people who genuinely care for us.

When I turned seven years old, I transferred to Assumption Elementary School which shared the same campus with Assumption High School where my older brother, Reggie, went. I no longer have a 'yaya,' so I walked with my brother to the Cathedral's patio (turned into a parking lot) where the school buses were waiting. My six-foot-four-inch-tall brother was a senior high school student, and I was in first grade. Each day, I struggled to catch up with a tall teenager with big walking strides.   I had to run to catch him and make sure not to fall into a ditch again. I would often have to ask him to wait up so I could catch my breath. We had to walk quickly to avoid missing the school buses. Otherwise, we had to walk a long distance to my new school. One day, I tried something to make sure I wouldn't be left behind by my brother. And behold, I learned my second lesson on the road when I held my brother's hand as we walked, he adjusted his pace to mine as I too adjusted mine to his. Surprisingly, we started walking at the same pace.

Life's journey is not so much about competition but rather about companionship. The journey becomes much easier and happier when we walk hand in hand. Life was never meant to be traveled alone. We travel together with companions. Life journeys are also about relationships – building and nurturing beautiful relationships on the road. Indeed, there are some roads that lead to somewhere, but there are also some roads that lead to someone.

Life lessons can be learned best on the roads of life. These roads may sometimes be the physical road structures we travel each day. However, more often than not, they are the daily challenges and battles that we face each day. My faith in my faithful God, my love for my loving wife, my joy in my wonderful family, and my trust in my trustworthy friends have been my staff when life's roads became treacherous and overwhelming.

Over the years, my family and friends have shared their stories with me, which have enriched my theological and philosophical reflections on my life journey. I wrote this book, "Some Roads Lead to Somewhere. Some Roads Lead to Someone", to share these reflections with those who have at one time been my travelling companions and to those who are still on life's roads with me. I believe they have been used and are still being used by God to shape me to be the kind of person He wants me to be.

May all who read my reflections be blessed in many wonderful ways.

Dr. Rodel Aguas
Raspeburg, Maryland, USA
October 22, 2024

Chapter One

Some Roads Lead to Tears and Laughter

Sometimes we take the road that leads to the valley of tears and sometimes the road that leads to the mountains of laughter.

****

God might be used as a drug to forget or escape from our responsibilities of facing and solving our problems, problems that we created.

****

Life is beautiful. Our goal in life is not only to be happy but also to be good. When you love life, it will love you back.

****

Not everyone will like you. This shouldn't be a problem because what others think about you is their problem, not yours. The opinion of other people does not define who you are. Nobody can define you better than you.

****

Only those who are filled with hatred will be offended by a beautiful smile.

****

The sunset reminds me that today's troubles will pass and that a new day will dawn. One of the best forms of self-care that I know is choosing to be very happy despite a very bad day.

****

Our scars remind us not only that we have been wounded, but also that we have been healed.

****

God does not control examination results so you will pass, nor does He make your favorite sports team win the championship game.

But He can give you the serenity to accept failure and defeat, the wisdom to discover your weaknesses and turn them into strength, and the determination to succeed and to win next time.

****

Remember that truth will hurt but it will also set you free. Truth is an ally of freedom.

****

It is foolish to pursue something that you may never have but it is more tragic to live the rest of your life regretting that you never tried.

****

Find a good reason to be happy every day. If you are in darkness, try searching for a ray of light. If there is none, then imagine the sun shining on you. If you are feeling sad, find a simple reason to smile... think about past victories. But if you are unable to find a reason to smile, then smile for no reason. It is much easier to smile rather than to frown and to drown yourself in the pit of self-pity.

****

Are you unemployed and are the bills piling up? Look at your feet, can they walk? Look at your hands, can they work? If they can, then start to walk and work. Imagine people without feet, without hands, and yet they find a reason to free themselves from the paralysis of self-pity.

If you are drowning in the sea of anxiety, stop struggling and try to float. The sea that should have drowned you can be used to move you to safety.

And if you have a broken heart, shed tears if you must, but also celebrate with laughter for the wrong person is gone and the right one will come.

****

Happiness inhabits the lives of those who choose to be happy.

****

Never allow bitterness and hate to consume you. There's no peace in an angry heart.

****

We are meant to be Easter Sunday people not Good Friday people. We are a people of hope and never of despair.

****

I still remember the days of praying in tears for the blessings I now have.

****

The chaos and disorder that spread havoc in one's life are oftentimes the dramatic prelude to the peace and harmony of a better life.

****

It is in that darkness, loneliness, and struggles inside the dreaded cocoon where something beautiful and wonderful is formed in secret.

****

True sadness comes from seeking everlasting happiness from things that cannot last.

****

Where is God Amid Our Sufferings?

The setting for the 2005 film, "Beyond the Gates" (also titled, "Shooting Dogs"), is a Salesian Catholic high school in Kigali, Rwanda which has turned into a refugee center by fleeing minority Tutsi people. The civil war in Rwanda has resulted into the mass killings of the Tutsi by the majority Hutu-led government and Hutu militias. Dead bodies of Tutsis and their supporters lay scattered on village roads and fields.

In the final scenes of the film, the Hutu militias have surrounded the school as the small unit of the United Nations (UN) Peacekeeping Force evacuates foreign nationals leaving behind the helpless Tutsi refugees. Joe Connor (Hugh Dancy) is a young British teacher in that school who witnessed the sufferings and genocide of the Tutsi. Though he has grown to love the Tutsi people, he finds that he is just as helpless as they are. He is, himself, consumed by a terrible fear of dying in the hands of the machete -

wielding Hutu militias. Now boarded in the UN truck, he notices Father Christopher (John Hurt), a Catholic priest, among the Tutsi people who crowded around the trucks. He is surprised as well as burdened with guilt that he is also leaving behind the old European missionary, his friend and mentor. He quickly gets off the truck and rushes to the priest to convince him to board the truck. But he soon realizes that the priest has firmly made up his mind to stay behind with the Tutsi people. He smiles at Joe and comforts him that he does not need to feel guilty for his decision to leave Rwanda. Then he explains to Joe why he made the opposite decision to stay behind:

"You asked me, Joe, 'Where is God in everything that is happening here ... in all the suffering.' I know exactly where He is. He's right here ... His love is here ... more intense and more profound than I have ever felt. And my heart is here, Joe, my soul. And if I leave, I think I may not find it again."

We may, like Joe, ask also, "Where is God when His people are suffering?"

God is nowhere far from His suffering people. He does not abandon us in our sufferings. For He is "Emmanuel" – God is with us. He is with us in our suffering, assuring us of His love. His presence does not take away the pain but transforms it into a meaningful and sanctifying tool to achieve His greater divine plan.

Chapter Two

Some Roads Lead to the Heart

Our heartaches and broken hearts remind us that our hearts belong to no one but to the One who first loved us.

****

Strange and powerful, this thing is called "love". While it can make you laugh, it can also make you cry.

****

Forgetting someone special is not only difficult ... it is impossible.

****

When you love someone, share your true feelings with authenticity and vulnerability. Life is too precious to conceal the beauty of your emotions. And if a relationship must come to an end, explain your reasons with kindness and transparency. Life is too short to stay in a relationship that lacks genuine connection. Embracing honesty may be challenging, but it will ultimately liberate you and bring profound peace of mind.

****

Embracing marriage as a personal choice, driven solely by genuine love which empowers individuals to create a fulfilling union. Recognizing that happiness is a shared responsibility, couples can cultivate a joyful relationship by prioritizing each other's well-being. By acknowledging that happiness and love are gifts that multiply when shared, individuals can approach marriage with optimism and a deep understanding of its transformative potential.

Happiness is something that you cannot find in marriage. Happiness is something you bring into marriage. For happiness, like love, is something you can only have by giving it away.

****

Do not enter a marriage unless the only reason for getting married is true love. For true love is something that only the heart can recognize.

****

Marriage is a lifetime commitment. Financial readiness is a very important factor to consider because even if you are in love, you also need to pay the bills.

****

I strongly believe it is important for both lovers to have their own careers before getting married. A career will provide each with a cushion to fall back if the marriage falls apart.

****

It is foolish to pursue a relationship that was doomed to end from the very start. Before starting or ending a relationship of the heart, it is wise to seek the help of the Author of Marriage, Himself, God, and to seek also the counsel of the holy.

****

Seek a relationship where you are always at peace with God.

****

To love and yet not trust exhausts a relationship to its sad ending.

****

A third party is an indication of a troubled marriage.

****

Fidelity in marriage brings abundant blessings while infidelity brings nothing but troubles.

****

Love makes lovers one but still different.

****

Love is forever. If it isn't forever, it never was love after all.

****

I do not envy the immortal gods but the mortal lovers whose love is eternal.

****

The need to love oneself is something that the generous nature of love would require every lover to recognize and respect in the beloved.

****

Love requires us to choose what is right, even if this will break our hearts. Be comforted however with the knowledge that it is only through our brokenness that light can penetrate and dispel the darkness that envelops us.

****

To love is to risk it all; to defy reason; to take the pains; to accept the blame; to lose friends; to embrace death willingly; and yet to be so happy without regrets all in the name of love. For to love is to risk it all ... yes ... all for the good of the beloved.

****

I strongly agree with the teachings of the Church that sex is procreative. It was designed primarily for the survival of the human species. That part of our body designed for sex is called the reproductive system. Theologically, it is a means whereby the image of God is transferred from one human species to another. Sex is also pleasurable. It is sensually satisfying, and thus it is desirable. To seek the pleasures that sex brings is an indication of our nature as sexual or sensual beings. Sex is intimate. It is an expression of the profound knowledge the couple have for each other. It must freely be given and freely received. Sex that is forced upon is not intimate, and therefore it is not pleasurable. Since sex entails intimacy and responsibility, it is an act of commitment. Marriage is the institution wherein this commitment can be truly nurtured.

****

There are two kinds of love, according to the philosopher, René Descartes: first, "compassionate love" which involves the desire to seek the good of the beloved and second, "lustful love", which involves the desire to seek the beloved as good for oneself.

Both kinds of love can bring happiness to the lover: the first through the act of giving, and the latter through the act of receiving. Compassionate love when sanctified becomes ministry, and lustful love when sanctified becomes matrimony.

If love hurts, then lustful love will hurt the most because it is painful when something you value the most is taken away from you.

It is different, however, with compassionate love. Because you have already given everything away, what else can hurt you if you have nothing more to lose?

****

Some love stories are meant, to be lived, to be written, to be treasured, but none at all to be forgotten. For love is a beautiful story created by God who is Love.

****

Fall in love with someone who does not only love you but who can also make you learn to fall in love with yourself.

A Wedding Story

As they watched the bridal march, the Archbishop and two priests waited on the altar. When the bride met the groom, the young priest turned to the older priest and spoke. "Father, look at the bride, she is so beautiful. But look at the groom, he is not that ... handsome. Sigh ... love is blind indeed." The older priest giggled and replied, "No, Father. Love is not blind. Lovers are the ones who are blind." Both priests laughed, which annoyed the good old Archbishop who heard the two priests talking behind him. He motioned for them to come closer to him and told them, "Fathers, love is not blind, nor are the

23

lovers." Actually, we are the ones who are blind to the love that brought this couple to the Sacrament of Matrimony. The two priests stepped back in humility and finally saw the wedding in the true light of true love that sees nothing else but beauty.

Chapter Three

Some Roads Lead to School

Nicholas was the typical teacher's worst nightmare at daytime in school. But I refused to believe in this and started believing in him instead. I gave him my trust and respect and so did he to me. Slowly he showed signs of being a respectful and responsible student. Now he is the leader of one of the "learning groups" in our class. We cannot give up on our "problem" students just because they are annoying and different. Remember the saying: "crayons though broken can still color." This is the magic … of teaching.

****

A world without teachers will be a world filled with cheaters. Teachers are the champions of truth and righteousness. Behind every great leader is the shadow of a great teacher.

****

Teachers do not give grades, we report them. This is the reason why those cards are called "Report Cards" not "Gift Cards".

******

Grades do not measure our students' intelligence. It measures instead the effort that they have exerted to use their intelligence to become great students.

******

The only respect I demand from my students is that they pass my subject. Any disrespectful behavior is disrespect not on me but on themselves, their families, and their people.

******

Kindness as a teaching strategy hasn't been explored. For kindness creates a safe learning environment which enables children to freely engage with their hearts and minds in peace.

******

My job is to teach my students not to please them. That is how I kept my inner peace.

****

When you love your students, they will eventually love you back.

****

When teaching becomes not just a job but also a source of joy — it becomes a refuge where you experience peace within yourself and in your work.

****

As educators, we have a profound impact on our students, extending far beyond the knowledge we impart. By being our authentic selves, we show our students the value of empathy, compassion, and kindness, leaving a lasting impression that transcends academics.

Our students are more likely to recall how we made them feel, rather than what we taught them, and they learn valuable lessons by observing how we conduct ourselves.

****

What kind of a teacher is Jesus? Jesus is patient. Jesus is kind. He does not envy. He does not boast. He is not proud. He does not dishonor others. He is not self-seeking. He is not easily angered. He keeps no record of wrongs. He does not delight in evil but rejoices with the truth. He always protects, always trusts, always hopes, always perseveres. Jesus never fails. (1 Corinthians 13: 4 – 8)

****

A Hungry Student

I had once the opportunity to teach second grade pupils in a public school in a poor neighborhood in Baltimore City, Maryland. It was a cold morning and the kids were working on their first reading assignment. While monitoring the progress of each student, I noticed a little girl seated by the window who was crying. I approached her, pulled a chair, and sat next to her. Then I began to inquire why she was crying.

I asked with a soft voice, "Why are you crying?"

She replied in between sobs, "I am hungry."

"Didn't you eat breakfast at the cafeteria?"

"No, I came late."

"Why were you late?"

"My mom was still sleeping when I woke up."

"Why was your mom ..."

"She works in the evening .... I am hungry."

"Oh okay, I have a McDonald's cheeseburger in my lunch bag. It's yours"

She was still crying when I went to my table to get my lunch bag. I quickly went back to her and gave her my sandwich, apple juice, and tissue to wipe off her tears. She stopped crying, wiped her tears, and began to eat. I left her and went around the classroom to monitor the other kids. Then I came back to check on her. "How are you now? Are you still hungry?" I asked. "No, I am fine. Thank you," she replied. I watched her until she finished eating. Then I asked. "Do you need anything else?" She looked at me with her big light brown eyes, gave a very beautiful smile, and said, "Yes." I got curious and asked, "What is it?" Then she reached out to me and ... hugged me.

It was then my turn to cry.

Chapter Four

Some Roads Lead to Movies

Jesus Christ Superstar (Film 1973)
Reflection on the Role of Mary Magdalene

The writer of Jesus Christ Superstar must have been confused, like most of us, with the role of Mary Magdalene in the life of the historical Jesus. First, Mary Magdalene is not the prostitute who anointed Jesus with an expensive perfume in the Gospel. Neither is she the woman caught in adultery and brought to Jesus for judgment but whom He forgave instead. Mary Magdalene was a woman who was possessed by evil spirits whom Jesus healed (Luke 8:2; Mark 16:9). From then on, she became a follower of Jesus and one of the financial supporters of His public ministry (Luke 8:3). Mary Magdalene should instead remind us of how Jesus honored women by recognizing their significant role in His mission - something that was unlikely during those times where the male dominated the religious arena. Mary Magdalene and the other women were with Jesus throughout His public ministry including His crucifixion when all the male disciples were in hiding (except John). It was also to these women that Jesus chose to appear first in His resurrected body. He names only one woman there present - Mary Magdalene, to announce His resurrection. Mary is honored as a saint by the Church with a feast day on July 22. It is also wrong to say that she is the patroness of prostitutes because she was never a prostitute and why should prostitutes have a patroness in the first place? I think her love and loyalty to Jesus should be emulated instead. She followed Jesus to His Crucifixion because she understood His mission and how important this was to Him. Although she was powerless and helpless in preventing the death of Jesus, she risked it all just to be there, to be with Jesus so that He will not have to bear the agony of dying alone; to console her Lord and Master, that He still had friends present as He breathes His last. I think Mary Magdalene (and Mary, the mother of Jesus) should be the patroness of those who are suffering and dying alone that they may be consoled with the thought that God has not abandoned them.

****

Breaking Dawn (2012)

Reflection on Love and Life

in the Light of Mortality and Immortality

The Twilight Saga finale, Breaking Dawn Part 1 (2011) and Breaking Dawn Part II (2012), brings to light not really the conflict between good and evil but rather the predicaments of an immortal love and a mortal life. The film tackles the problem of fear and the anxiety we face over beautiful romantic and filial relationships that eventually must end not because love ends but because life ends. That is why the marriage vow ends with the words: "till death do us apart."

Edward Cullen and Bella Swan decided to get married to seal their love for each other even though the former is an immortal (as a vampire) and the latter is mortal (as a human). They face the fear and anxiety that they will not be together forever. The mortal spouse will have to die someday. This fear becomes true when Bella gets pregnant and imperils her life. Edward finds himself helpless to help his wife survive the danger of giving birth. In his desperation to save his wife, he turns her into an immortal (a vampire). Their child, Renesmee, survives and Bella becomes immortal.

Their fear and anxiety do not end there. They learn that their daughter is mortal. She is going to die. And worse, she is growing up fast. Turning her into an immortal was not an option, for this might kill her instead.

Things became worse when the Volturi, the largest coven of vampires, who enforce vampire laws in the world, are misinformed that the daughter of Edward and Bella has been turned into a vampire. For them a child vampire is uncontrollable and dangerous to their secret world. They decide and embark to kill the child and the Cullen clan.

The Cullens face the Volturi with the help of other vampires from around the world to convince them that the child is not a vampire. The bloodbath is averted when Alice, a Cullen with a gift of precognition, shows the Volturi that a bloody encounter between them will lead to the defeat and annihilation of the Volturi. The fear on the nature of Renesmee is resolved when Nahuel, a 150-year-old vampire, proves to the Volturi that a crossbreed like himself (between a human and vampire) pose no threat to the secret world of the vampires.

Upon learning this, the fear and anxiety of Edward and Bella of losing their daughter to mortality is abated. Love and life become forever.

Of course, in real life this is not possible. We all fall in love, but we will have to depart in death someday. American singer Jim Croce realized this when his son was born. How he wished happy family moments will never have to end with death. And so, he wrote the beautiful song, "Time in Bottle." When his son turned two years old, Jim died in an airplane crash. The Filipino song "Sana'y Wala Nang Wakas" (*I Wish There Was No End*) depicts this painful desire that good things like romantic love, family life and friendships will not have to end with inevitable death. This is such a sad human reality - we all have to leave each other when death comes. It is therefore evident that in our human nature there is a longing to achieve immortality in love and in life.

Christianity is a religion that gives us hope that good things will last forever. God sent His Son to become human and showed us that we can recapture our immortality again through faith in Him. " For God so loved the world that he gave his only Son, so that everyone who believes in him might not perish but may have eternal life." John 3:16.

Love and life do not end in death. Death is simply an essential part of the process of transformation of these beautiful human experiences into perfection ... into forever.

Thus, we do not have to be bitten by a vampire to become immortal. We must believe in Jesus Christ and follow Him in the journey to forever.

****

Elysium (Film 2013)
Reflection on the Meaning of True Greatness

The purpose of this review is to present Gospel values or themes found in secular movies like Elysium. This is based on the premise that evangelization involves also the recognition of elements of culture which are consistent with the teachings of Jesus Christ that can help us understand better the mysteries of God.

The Gospel values/themes that I found in Elysium are the following:

1. Salvation is for everyone.

Director Neill Blomkamp's latest science fiction film, Elysium, presents two classes of people: the rich and the poor. The rich live in a man-made space station which was built to preserve their peaceful and luxurious way of life. The poor, on the other hand, live on earth which is overpopulated and cursed with widespread crime, poverty and diseases. Thus, they are desperate to go to Elysium which has successfully eradicated diseases through its advanced medical technology and care. However, anti - immigration laws are strictly enforced in Elysium to protect the pristine lifestyle of its citizens.

It is interesting to note why the man - made space station was called "Elysium." Elysium is a Latinization of the Greek word "Ἠλύσιον" - Elysion. In Greek mythology, it is actually the name of the blissful dwelling place of the souls of the blessed:

heroes and virtuous men and women in the afterlife. Elysium or Elysian Fields is the ancient Greek's perception of paradise or heaven. In Neill Blomkamp's Elysium, it is a man - made heaven for the world's blessed - the wealthy and Earth is for the damned - the world's poor. Salvation in this film therefore is a blissful life that is free from the stench of crime, poverty, and disease. But it is reserved only for the rich. Damnation, on the other hand, is deprivation of salvation which is the lot of the poor. But according to Christian teaching, salvation is for everyone. God ... "wants all people to be saved and to come to a knowledge of the truth "(1Timothy 2:4). Salvation is total liberation from all forms of evil which alienates us from God and His eternal life. It begins in this life and is completed in the afterlife. Therefore, whatever will set us free from any evil here on earth must be made available to all mankind. This salvation is being offered to all mankind through Jesus Christ. "For God so loved the world that he gave his one and only Son, that whoever believes in him shall not perish but have eternal life " (John 3:16).

The film ends with the action-packed elimination of the severe anti - immigration laws with the heroic sacrifice of Max de Costa (Matt Damon), an ex-convict in Los Angeles turned hero. His self-sacrifice allows the people of Earth to become citizens of Elysium enabling them among others to avail advanced Med - Pods putting an end to all diseases on Earth.

2. We are all destined for greatness.

At the start of the film, young, orphaned Max De Costa who is overwhelmed by the reality of poverty and the literal huge gap between the rich (in Elysium) and the poor (on Earth), is consoled by an old Catholic nun from the orphanage. It is interesting to note that Director Blomkamp still sees the survival of the Catholic religion in 2154 and associates the Church with the poor instead of the rich who apparently have become godless. Max envies the beauty of Elysium as seen from Earth, but the old nun corrects his impression and gives him a pendant with the photo of the beautiful blue planet earth as seen by the citizens of Elysium. She tries to heal Max's broken self- image by telling him that he will do something great for mankind someday. Max of course, does not understand how someone like him, cursed with a lot of poverty, can do something great for mankind.

Perhaps we, too, who are not highly educated, financially successful, and popular as celebrities, could do something great for mankind or at least for ourselves and families. It looks impossible from inside and out to be destined for greatness when our lot is in the pit of poverty, disease and oppression. But these should not prevent us from asserting respect for our human dignity and fulfilling our duty to do what is just and good for human society whatever our status in life may be. Max became a felon and was released from prison on parole. To make his situation worse, he met an industrial accident in the factory he works for, gets exposed to high levels of radiation, and has only five days to live. This is not a good picture of one destined for greatness. However, this sad sorry situation ignites his childhood desire to go to Elysium, infiltrate it, and have himself cured with the Med - Pod. He becomes determined and focuses his efforts to reach Elysium at all costs. He gets his chance to go to Elysium when he is made to steal important corporate data from John Carlyle's brain, CEO of Armadyne Corporation, which is the contract builder of Elysium. He learns that the stolen corporate information could change the entire program of Elysium allowing the people of Earth to become citizens. He also learns that the process of extracting the data from his brain would kill him. He chooses to sacrifice himself and extracts the data from his brain to the main computer of Elysium which changed the entire program allowing the people of Earth to become citizens. A citizen from Earth becomes President and humanitarian missions are sent immediately from Elysium to Earth bringing Medi-Pods to cure and end diseases on Earth. The prophesy of the old Catholic nun came true. Max did something great for all mankind.

All men and women are destined for greatness. This is because each one of us has the quality of goodness inherent in our nature as human beings - as creatures of God who is all - good. The Sacred Scriptures affirms that we have godlike qualities in our nature because we were all created in the image and likeness of God (cf. Genesis 1:27). The quality of goodness in us must however be manifested in good deeds for the common good. When the Son of God assumed human form, he manifested the quality of goodness in the human nature. The Sacred Scriptures say that "he went about doing good" (Acts 10:38). We, therefore, must manifest, like Jesus Christ, that goodness in our nature by choosing to do good and persevere in doing good. "Let us not become weary in doing good, for at the proper time we will reap a harvest if we do not give up." Galatians 6:9).

Thus, we achieve greatness only when we manifest the goodness in us for the common good.

"Batman versus Superman: Dawn of Justice"
(Film 2016)

Reflections on God and the Perception of Evil

It is interesting that this movie includes the theological problems on God and the perception of evil in its plot.

1. The Question on God

Superman, a name coined by the US military to identify this powerful alien being, is considered as a god by most people especially by Lex Luthor. Belief in the existence of God is thus openly discussed in the plot of this movie as a basic need of men to recognize a supreme being, someone more powerful than them. Luthor, on the other hand, questions such common belief: "God is all - good. But is he all-powerful?" This mockery arises from the discovery that kryptonite minerals can kill the kryptonite cells of the "gods." Luthor also discovers that gods have a weakness other than kryptonite - a woman. In the case of Superman, it was not Lois Lane but his mother, Martha.

This made me think that Jesus Christ may have a weakness too - His mother, Mary.

2. The Perception of Evil

The conflict between Batman and Superman stems from their own perception of evil specifically on who is evil. For Batman, Superman is evil because of the death and destruction his duel with the Kryptonians has brought to Metropolis. Since he is being pursued by renegade Kryptonians, he poses a threat to humankind. Batman also fears that if Superman's enormous power goes unchecked this will also pose danger to our world. On the other hand, for Superman, Batman is evil as vigilante who takes matters into his own hands as judge, jury, and executioner. Thus, he must be stopped because he has caused terror and chaos in Gotham City with his vigilante activities. From this conflict between the two superheroes, Lex Luthor sees an evil opportunity to end them both. This will allow him to pursue his evil designs without any hindrance from his enemies. For him, Batman and Superman are evil ... not him. Evil it seems is perceived as the opposite of who we are. But in the later part there is a mention of the goodness in humanity that is worth saving. Thus, evil in the end is the opposite of good.

This made me think that every human being does not have to be a superhero to do the right thing. Every one of us is called to save the world from evil. We do not have to be superheroes to do that. We simply must be persons who go about doing good.

****

"La La Land" (Film 2016)

Reflections on True Love

This is a love story between Sebastian (Ryan Gosling) and Mia (Emma Stone) whose first meeting was in a California traffic jam. Sebastian is a struggling jazz pianist while Mia was a struggling actress. It seems that destiny has brought them together in the down moments of their lives and eventually they fall in love with each other. They make a good team enjoying each other. Then, finally each one finds an opportunity to make their dreams come true. And this is where they chose to part ways to pursue their dreams. Sebastian fulfills his dream of owning a successful jazz bar and Mia becomes a famous actress. After five years they meet again at Sebastian's jazz bar. This is the most heartbreaking and most beautiful part of the movie. Sebastian plays a sad jazz piece on the piano sending Mia the sad message on how he wished it was the two of them together instead. But Mia is now happily married and has a little daughter. They look at each other for the last time. They smile and gesture each other with an assuring nod that everything is alright ... happy to say goodbye and move on. There are a lot of lessons to be learned from this movie. I would like to share three:

a. Some people that you love are meant to be in your heart but not in your life.

b. We must take the risk of choosing whom we love over what we love. We may one day regret having not tried.

c. An opportunity for true love comes to us so rare. If we miss it, it may never come again.

"Beauty and the Beast" (Film 2017)

Reflections on Appearance, Love, and Women

The story, though criticized for its controversial insinuations on the homosexual character and moments of LeFou, Gaston's sidekick, is still full of beautiful moral lessons.

Among these are the following:

1. Do not judge people by their external appearance. It is bad to treat others unkindly and unjustly just because they are different or just because they do not meet our standards of what is good and beautiful. The prince ridiculed his guest and her gift

because she was old, ugly, and poorly dressed for the party. It turned out the old woman was a beautiful, enchanted lady who cast a spell on him turning him into an ugly beast.

2. Sometimes we must let go of those whom we love to show how much we love them. Love is not always about holding on, sometimes it is also about letting go. Love requires freedom for one who is not free cannot be happy. True love desires the happiness of the beloved. Beast let go of Belle because he loved her, and she returned to him because they were meant for each other.

3. Love is the strongest force in the universe that can reverse the effects of evil. It can turn the dark and gloomy winters of our lives into beautiful and amazing springtime. Though dehumanized by the evil of this world, love can get us in touch again with our dignity as human persons. It is our capacity to love that distinguishes us from beasts. Beast gradually recovered his human values when he learned to love again.

4. The world needs more women who share the values of Belle - who can transform the beastly ways of men back into their loving human nature again. Many men like the beastly Gaston often resort to violence - make wars that create widows, orphans, and refugees. The world needs more women like Belle who value family, education, decency, and peace. The role of women in social transformation cannot be underestimated and should be promoted. The training of women with positive values begins in the home.

****

God's Revelation of Himself in Movies

My older brother Ruben and I walked on our village road together several times when we were young. We went downtown together on Sundays to attend the 8:00 a.m. Mass. After the mass, we would go to the movie houses and look at their displays of colored still photos and posters of the "now showing", "next picture" and "coming soon" movies. It's like going on window shopping for movies. We called this "karter" in our local dialect. Each movie house during that time was a separate building unlike the movies houses today which are located in a shopping mall or housed in a single building. My fondness for movies was influenced by my brother who often took me to the movies when he had money. When I was old enough to go to movie houses by myself, I sold empty bottles and metal scraps to pay for my movie tickets and snacks. I went to see movies for entertainment but as I got older, I didn't just watch movies. I began to see their connection to my life and between the reel world and the real world.

And as my faith in Jesus Christ deepened, my perception of evangelization also deepened. Evangelization, I began to realize, is not merely the process of transferring Christian truths to a culture but it also involves the recognition that there are Gospel truths embedded in a culture. These could be used to enrich our understanding of the mysteries of

God. Movies are part of the culture of modern societies today. Thus, it is the purpose of the film reviews that I made to unearth Gospel themes and truths in movie or films. These can be used as tools in evangelization, catechesis, and in the formation of contemporary theology.

My walks with my brother to the church and the movie houses on Sundays led me to a deeper relationship with Jesus Christ. God indeed works in mysterious ways. Indeed, every path leads to Thee.

Chapter Five

Some Roads Lead to Me

Alone ... I find myself.

****

The journey to self-discovery begins when you realize you are lost and have to find yourself.

****

It is not necessary for you to agree with yourself all the time. Sometimes you have to do the opposite of what you want to do in order to stay out of trouble. Sometimes we have to say 'no' to ourselves to say 'yes' to God. Our Lord Jesus and the Christian mystics refer to this as self-denial.

****

I give because I love. But when my gift is taken for granted and my sincerity is doubted, I step back and become a wiser person.

Be authentic, especially in the face of persecution. You do not have to conform to the standards of your detractors, but instead you can be conformed to the standards of Christ Jesus.

****

Be true to yourself. Be honest with yourself. And you will be happy.

****

If you have a bad attitude, then your beauty is all but a lie, a mask hiding the ugliness within.

****

Sometimes when I get lost and confused, I don't look for answers. I eat ice cream.

****

What is most crucial is not the path before us nor the path behind us but where we are right now.

****

Our strength and blessings are always at the service of the weak and underprivileged.

****

You may make mistakes. You may lose some battles. And at the end of the day, you can only trust a few. But the loyalty of a few is all you need to achieve victory.

****

Never hurry to succeed. Everything is designed to have its own pace and timeframe. We achieve success through the pathway of patience and perseverance.

****

Who am I really? Throughout this retreat God has been reminding me of my dignity, my esteemed status not only as a creature but as His child and His friend. Not unless this sinks deep into the sacred recesses of my entire being can I truly know, understand, and accept my purpose in life. God created me for a purpose and likewise made me His child and His friend to affirm the significance and seriousness of this purpose. My existence therefore is linked to my Creator who is not only my Father but also my friend. Jesus was always conscious of who He was and focused on the purpose for which He came here on earth. I think this is what God wanted me to imitate if I really wanted to attain fulfillment and experience true happiness in my life. I cannot achieve anything significant in life if I am not at peace with my own identity and purpose. It is who I am really that makes me who I am supposed to be.

****

What does God want me to do? God delights in me and loves me deeply because I am not only a creature, but His child and friend. This is the reason why He desires me to be happy. Therefore, God wants me to do what makes me truly happy. This is the challenge I must face: to figure out what will truly make me happy. He has witnessed my tears shed in my quiet struggles. He comprehends the unspoken pains and sufferings that are harbored in my heart. He understands my weaknesses and tendencies to fall into temptations. He is not the kind of God who eagerly waits to catch me doing something wrong and punishes me each time I make a mistake. He is God who is prepared and willing to forgive me if I fail to be strong against the barrage of temptations that the Devil has prepared to break and crush me with. Maybe this is the reason why God is so close to the crushed and brokenhearted. He will not let us remain crushed and broken, He will rebuild us and make us stronger than before. He will not stop until we become perfect.

A Late-Night Call

One evening I had a call from my former classmate in high school. It had already been decades since I heard from him. It was actually the first time he called me. We had been classmates since elementary and high school, except in our senior high school year. We were classmates, but we were not that close as friends. He was from a rich family, and I was from a poor family. We seldom spoke, even if we were classmates. Naturally, it was a surprise for me that he called me. I think that night, he needed someone who would listen to him. Yes, just to listen to him.

After exchanging pleasantries and sharing our high school memories with each other, he finally opened up his soul to me. He had been suffering from deep depression for a while. This was in spite of having a wonderful family of his own, successful businesses, and all the luxuries that his immense wealth could buy. There was emptiness in his life that he did not understand. This had affected his health condition, requiring him to take a regimen of assorted medicines and frequent trips to the hospital. He was sad ... sad. He was scared ... petrified.

Then he told me this story. One day, on his way to check his business operations, he passed by an old gasoline station. He was compelled to stop for reasons he didn't know. He then got out of his car and approached an old house next to the gasoline station. This house was familiar to him. It was the house where he grew up... his home as a child. As he looked at his childhood home, happy memories of his family and his childhood came back to him. Although tears fell from his eyes, these were tears of joy. He then asked me if I knew why tears of joy fell from my eyes that day. I did not respond and there was a brief peaceful silence. He finally broke that silence and said, "It was because at that moment when I was looking at my childhood home, I found myself again." I felt peace within me that years of painkillers never gave me. I was reminded of who I really am, and I experienced incredible joy. Finding myself has made me realize that what truly matters in life is not material wealth, but family and friends.

Then he told me this story. One day, on his way to check his business operations, he passed by an old gasoline station. He was compelled to stop for reasons he didn't know. He then got out of his car and approached an old house next to the gasoline station. This house was familiar to him. It was the house where he grew up... his home as a child. As he looked at his childhood home, happy memories of his family and his childhood came back to him. Although tears fell from his eyes, these were tears of joy. He then asked me if I knew why tears of joy fell from my eyes that day. I did not respond and there was a brief peaceful silence. He finally broke that silence and said, "It was because at that moment when I was looking at my childhood home, I found myself again." I felt peace within me that years of painkillers never gave me. I was reminded of who I really am, and I experienced incredible joy. Finding myself has made me realize that what truly matters in life is not material wealth, but family and friends.

I completely agree with him that our true wealth is our family and friends because it is only with them, we can honestly be our true selves.

That same night, my former classmate and I became friends for the first time.

Chapter Six

Some Roads Lead Home

In the universe, I was alone, and You gave me family.

****

Home is a place where we love people, not merely things.

****

Teach your children to love Jesus Christ as their Lord and Savior, and they will honor and love you with their righteous life and take care of you in your old age.

****

When husband and wife fight each other, the children are the ones who hurt the most.

And when siblings fight each other, it is the parents who experience the greatest pain.

****

But when a family breaks apart, it is God who bears the most hurts and pains. Why? Because God Himself is part of the family too.

****

A son can become a good husband only when he sees his father loving his mother faithfully. He can become a good father only when he sees his father doing his very best to be one. A great society is possible when its families have good husbands and good fathers in it. If the husband is good, then the wife can focus more on her role in the family instead of worrying everyday about why her husband does not love her. And if the father is good, then the children would not have to think of running away from home and becoming problems of society.

****

There are two wonderful gifts we can give our children: one is roots, the other is wings. Strong roots will help them stand against the strong winds of life's storms. Powerful wings will make them tap turbulent winds soar up high above these storms.

****

There is a powerful and wonderful bond that exists between grandparents and their grandchildren. It is called ... "falling in love again".

****

Every child needs to be assured every day by their parents that they are loved and cared for. Otherwise, they will seek it elsewhere.

****

My child, never forget the two amazing people in your life. First, the woman who risked her life so that you would live. She is your queen ... your comforting companion in every pain in your life. Behold, she is your mother, and second, the man who taught you how to live victoriously. He is your king, your vigilant protector from the evils of this world. Behold, he is your father. They are not perfect, and neither are you. If you truly love them as you say you do, then honor and obey them so that you and your children will surely be blessed with long and happy lives.

****

Oftentimes, the deepest hurts and pains are experienced in the family. But family members get over these and get along with each other not because they forget, but because they forgive. Forgiveness is never about forgetting, for this is impossible and only God can forgive and forget. Forgiveness is not really something we do for others. It is more of something we do for ourselves. It is freeing oneself from memories that hurt us, so that when we remember them, we are not hurt anymore. The person who holds on to unforgiveness hurts the most. If you find it difficult to forgive, ask God to forgive through you, and you will have peace in your heart and pleasant dreams in your sleep.

65

Once upon a time there were no such things as gadgets, and children played in the beautiful fields instead of in a dark room alone. And yes, they were happy, healthy, and respectful ... once upon a time.

****

Indeed, it is the primary duty of parents to educate their children. The State and the Church merely help the parents to fulfill this task. Good manners and right conduct are supposed to be taught and learned first in the home. The school merely reinforces these. Yes, it takes a village to raise a child, but the responsibility of parenthood still rests primarily on the shoulders of the child's parents, not on the village.

****

You may make mistakes. You may lose some battles. And at the end of the day, you can only trust and depend on a few. But you should know deep down in your mind and heart that the loyalty of a few is all you need to achieve a decisive victory. They are your family and friends.

****

979 Santa Teresita Street

Our old house was located on a street that linked McArthur Highway and San Fernando Public Market. If you enter from McArthur Highway, it's the third house on the right. The first house is actually a small restaurant and store. The second house belonged to a lawyer who was a relative of my father. They were rich and were one of the few families who owned a car in our village. Our home was a renovated two –story wooden house with a decent yard where we had a mango tree, guava trees, star apple tree, banana trees, and lots of ornamental plants.

I had a lot of happy memories playing with my friends and cousins from our neighborhood. When we were not playing on the street, they sometimes came to play with me and my brothers in our yard. The first floor had the bare ground as floor and was called "lalam bale" (basement) which was used for storage. This was also where we played "bale balayan" (playhouse) with our cousins and friends. We also made tree houses, hunted for birds, and had picnics in our playhouses.

I had plenty of sad memories too in our home. When I was five years old, my mother died on her bed after succumbing to a brain tumor. We did her wake in our house for several days. I was too young to comprehend my first experience of death in our family and in our house. The second one happened when I became a teenager. When my brother died, we had another wake up in our house. He was only 28 years old at the time. He was gunned down with his friend by corrupt city police who claimed it was a mistaken identity. The third was when my grandmother died. She was a symbol of our family's unity and pride. Finally, my older brothers and sisters began getting married and moving with their spouses to raise their own families. My father remarried, and they moved to their new house as well. I felt as if everyone I loved was leaving me, and I felt sad.

Nonetheless I had many happy memories too in our home with my family. The prayers before our daily meals, that I helped set on the long table, strengthened our sense of family. Our family believed in this wisdom: "A family that prays together, stays together." We all prayed the rosary daily at twilight, which was led by our grandmother. After praying the rosary, we raced to see which sibling would first kiss the hand of our grandmother. Christmas Eve was a happy time as we shared the "noche buena" (Christmas eve meal), exchanged gifts, and played parlor games. During weekends, my bothers Reggie and Ruben played the guitar while my sisters and I would sing songs from "Jingle" (a song magazine). We did countless silly things like jokes with each other before we went to sleep on our designated "dase" (sleeping mats) in the living room.

I had my share of sadness as well as happiness in the home where I grew up. These are now but memories that I have come to make peace within my mind and in my heart. I have my own home now in another country, but I still long to return to 979 Santa Teresita Street someday.

Chapter Seven

Some Roads Lead to Heaven

In silence, we can listen ... and when we can listen in silence, we hear the soothing voice of God.

****

There was a time when theologians learned their Theology on bent knees at the feet of Jesus; when Gospel truths were taught in the streets and in the marketplace; when the students sought were the sinners and outcasts of society; when the theologian was more of a passionate lover than a scholar obsessed with academic excellence; and when the heart and soul of Theology was Jesus ...

And only Jesus.

****

Our prayers are answered not only because we have prayed devotedly, but also because of the fervent prayers of those who love us.

****

Don't be sad if you didn't get the miracle you prayed for today. This is God's way of telling you that your miracle was meant for the perfect day, but it isn't today.

If you pray for rain, God will first provide you with an umbrella before sending the rain. Don't give up ... He isn't going to give up on you.

****

I can smile at the stormy seas because the God who calms the storms is in my boat.

****

On Christmas Day, we are like the shepherds who must leave our flock in the fields, whatever these may symbolize, so may worship Jesus Christ.

****

Christmas reminds us that ... We can still hope even if the stench of hopelessness surrounds us. Even if the terror of hatred lurks around us, we can still experience love even if we are afraid.

And behold, we can also have joy, even if we are overwhelmed by sadness.

****

Peace can be found even if we hear of distant wars. We have hope, love, joy, and peace because we have a Savior. His Name is Jesus.

He is Emmanuel – God is with us.

****

When I was in trouble, God rushed to my rescue. He restored what I had lost and repaired what I had broken. He stood up to my enemies and put them to shame. Ah ... He did more than these things... He removed me from the road that leads to Hell and brought me back to the road that leads to Heaven.

****

If God is your Father, and He is my father, what then is our relationship? We are siblings - brothers and sisters. Jesus revolutionized the image of redeemed humanity as a family under the Fatherhood and Friendship of God. There is perhaps no religion other than Christianity which dares to intimately address and approach God as Father and Friend. All that we have is given to us not as a mere privilege but as a right (John 1:12) God Himself has given this to us. This is a right that not even angels enjoy. But it is a right that we have oftentimes neglected or forgotten. We have missed many times the joy of prayers being answered because we have not approached God with the trust and expectation of a child. We often think of Him as a genie who gives wishes or as a potential donor who gives donations. God is our Father, and we are His children. Much deeper than this is the fact that we are His friends. The grace of answered prayers comes only from this kind of relationship.

****

If you desire God above anything, you will have everything. (Matthew 6:33)

****

God understands us ... perfectly and lovingly.

****

Never lose hope for we always have God
on our side.

****

There is a far better place than heaven that I
know of ... it is the loving embrace of God my Father
and my Best Friend forever.

****

God's goodness and protection go hand in
hand. For when He blesses us, He not only protects
the one that He has blessed, but also the blessings
that He has given.

****

How God Trains His Best Warriors

God trains His best warriors in the bitter
grounds of loneliness: Noah amid a worldwide flood;
Abraham migrating in a hostile foreign land; Moses
forcibly exiled in the desert; Elijah hiding in a cave at

Mount Horeb; Jesus spending forty days and nights in the desert; and Paul spending several years in different prisons.

There are battles that cannot be told and are better left untold. No one would understand these anyway. There are defeats that one must grieve alone and victories that can only be celebrated in silence.

The warrior raised by the hand of God must learn to suffer alone. It is in solitude that he develops a strong fighting heart so that wounded or broken it may be, it cannot be crushed. A strong fighting heart a warrior will need for beside it the enemy will build its camp. God Himself trains His warriors .... Breaking them and wounding them ... to bring out their best so that the enemy trembles in fear at the very mention of their names.

And yes, the warrior must bear the pain of leaving behind even his beloved, for his battles require him to focus on one great love alone – his love for God

... his Creator, his Father, his Friend and his Destiny.

And God encompasses all those whom he loves for to love God is to love all.

Yes, in my heart, I truly believe all His warriors who have gone through Hell on earth and have remained faithful by His grace will surely go to Heaven.

Epilogue:

Some Roads Lead To Someone

How I Met My Brother

He is the Son of God, our Lord, and Savior. His name is Jesus Christ. These ideas about Jesus were taught to me by our Catholic family, the Catholic Church, and the Catholic school. That was how I knew things about Jesus. But knowing about someone and knowing someone are two different things. There were three events in my life on how I came to know Jesus.

The first event happened in my dormitory when I was in my first year in college in Manila. There was a strong typhoon and classes at all levels were suspended. My friend lent me a book, "The Mirror of Christ", which I decided to read since I had nothing better to do that day. It was the story of Saint Francis of Assisi, and I got absorbed in it. By evening, I finished reading the book. Suddenly, I experienced a different kind of joy and a longing which I could not explain. I began searching for Jesus.

The second event happened when I dropped out of the university and ran away from home. I had this very crazy idea to become a hermit in the mountains of Benguet, a northern province in the Philippines. I took a bus to Baguio City but when I arrived it rained very hard, so I had no choice but to seek shelter at my brother's house. I lied to him that I was there to attend a seminar. He called our parents, who were so worried looking for their "prodigal" son, to let them know that I was with him and they need not worry anymore. While in Baguio, I met Allen Ruiz, my classmate in high school, while I was walking along Session Road still figuring out how I could get to my destination. I told him the real reason why I came to Baguio City was to be a hermit.

He looked at me with deep curiosity and confusion figuring out what was really going on with me. Then he asked me why I wanted to be a hermit which I quickly answered, "I am searching for Jesus Christ!" He looked at me and gave me a reassuring smile that he understood ... and probably was relieved that his friend was not a nut case. He then took me to his apartment and there he told me about how he encountered Jesus through the Word of God. Then he asked me to pray with him so that God will enlighten me in my search. The next day, he introduced me to his pastor who read to me a small pamphlet, "The Four Spiritual Laws". Citing verses from the New Testament, he told me that God loves us and has wonderful plan for all of us. But we cannot experience this because of sin which separates us from God. To experience His love and plan, we must be sorry for our sins and accept Jesus as our personal Lord and Savior. These all made sense to me. He invited me to pray with him and on that day, I received Jesus in my heart as my King, Lord, and Savior. After praying, I felt the same joy that I felt in the college dormitory after reading "The Mirror of Christ". But something became much clearer to me. It became clear to me who Jesus really was because I finally met Him in faith. And yes, I did return home to my parents who welcomed me back with understanding and kindness and helped me grow in my faith in Jesus.

The third event happened in 2004 when I was in the emergency room in a hospital in Nevada, USA. I was brought in the ER due to fluids in my right lung which was on the verge of collapsing. I had suffered for a while from high fever and shortness of breath, and I needed to be confined immediately in the hospital. I asked the doctor in the emergency room what was wrong with me. And he bluntly told me, "It must be cancer." Immediately I was overwhelmed with depression, but I tried to be brave. Finally, they extracted the fluid in my right lung. It was green and I could see the nurse shaking her head. I started coughing which they said was caused by my lungs expanding again. There was no room available for me and so I was temporarily placed in what looked like an empty storeroom. After visiting hours were over, I was left alone, and I was really scared not knowing what would happen to me. I tried to pray but I could not utter any words into my prayer because I was gripped with sadness, fear, and coughing. Finally, I spoke a word ... "Jesus." Then I began singing in my head, "My life is in Your hands. You alone Lord are all that I have." This was a song we sang at Holy Mass at the university near the seminary when I was in college. I repeated that song over and over again in my head and I suddenly felt inexplicable peace. From that moment on, I never felt depressed, afraid, or alone. I knew that Jesus was with me – listening to me and taking care of me. While my doctors were racing against time to determine the cause of my rapidly failing health because of an unknown disease, I was immersed in that song that played over and over again in my head - "My life is in Your hands. You alone Lord are all that I have."

Because of my very serious condition pointing nowhere but to death, the chaplain wept as he gave me the Rite of Extreme Unction. For reasons I didn't know I was at peace most of the time as days of my failing health passed by. Finally, the results from the second laboratory in California came out. My right lung was infected with Coccidiodes Immitis, a pathogenic fungus. The doctors quickly changed their treatments, and I went through two major lung surgery called "Thoracotomy" with only 6% chance of survival. With the successful medical procedures and care and the thousands of prayers offered for my healing, I "miraculously" recovered and finally released from the hospital after 30 days. The doctors said I will be confined to a lifetime of medication to prevent the fungi from returning. But after a year, they investigated my lungs again and found not a single deadly fungus. I was declared healthy and was instructed to stop the medication.

So how did I meet my Brother?

In life's most unexpected moments, I encountered Him - during a stormy evening, while seeking refuge in a mountain city, and in a transformative near-death experience in a hospital. As I navigated life's crossroads in search of Jesus, I thought I had discovered Him, but the truth is, He was the one who found me first, embracing me with unconditional love.

Indeed, some roads lead to somewhere ... and some roads to lead to Someone.

Reunion with my friend, Angelo, whose phone call decades ago,
taught me the miracle of listening to people's stories of their journey in life.

Reunion with, Allen, my high school friend, who talked to me about his faith in Jesus Christ at a time when I was lost and confused during my troubled teenage life. This inspired me to follow the Way - our Jesus Christ, our Lord and Savior, our Brother and Friend.

My lovely mother took good care of us while
battling cancer silently. She passed away at the age of 39.
I was only 5 years old then.

The best awards for us teachers are those that come from
their students.

Sometimes Joy is spelled as F-A-M-I-L-Y.

Made in the USA
Middletown, DE
17 January 2026

27201326R00053